Practice ACTING, Becomes HABIT, Becomes LAW

Practice ACTING, Becomes HABIT, Becomes LAW

THOMAS BROWN

XULON PRESS

Xulon Press
555 Winderley Pl, Suite 225
Maitland, FL 32751
407.339.4217
www.xulonpress.com

© 2024 by Thomas Brown

590 Bergen Ave Jersey City, NJ 07304
201/ 667/6562
oldbrownclown@gmail.com

All rights reserved solely by the author. The author guarantees all contents are original and do not infringe upon the legal rights of any other person or work. No part of this book may be reproduced in any form without the permission of the author.

Due to the changing nature of the Internet, if there are any web addresses, links, or URLs included in this manuscript, these may have been altered and may no longer be accessible. The views and opinions shared in this book belong solely to the author and do not necessarily reflect those of the publisher. The publisher therefore disclaims responsibility for the views or opinions expressed within the work.

Unless otherwise indicated, Scripture quotations taken from the King James Version (KJV)–*public domain.*

Paperback ISBN-13: 979-8-86850-010-7
Ebook ISBN-13: 979-8-86850-011-4

This Book Is Dedicated To:

To Father God, the Lord Jesus Christ, My Savior, and the Father Gift to us, the Holy Ghost, and the Body of Christ for their dedication, commitment, for ministering, teaching, and prayers of the Word of faith.

Why I Wrote This Book

The Lord Jesus instructed me to write this book, with the teaching and understanding I receive from the Holy Ghost, who is leading and guiding me. The teaching was and *is* a big help in my life, and the life of others in the body of Christ. Many hidden mysteries of Scripture are revealed in this book. So many are struggling, lacking the understanding of how to rest in the Lord, to receive His forgiveness, and His healing power in all areas of their lives. *Isaiah 11:2 Amplified Bible, Classic Edition 2 says:*

> *And the Spirit of the Lord shall rest upon Him—the Spirit of wisdom and understanding, the Spirit of counsel and might, the Spirit of knowledge and of the reverential and obedient fear of the Lord—[3] And shall make Him of quick understanding, and His delight shall be in the reverential and obedient fear of the Lord. And He shall not judge by the sight of His eyes, neither decide by the hearing of His ears; [4] But with righteousness and justice shall He judge the poor and decide with fairness for the meek.*

I see these gifts by the Holy Ghost revealing themselves in my life. I have the gift to teach, and I believe in searching out different ways of teaching God's Word of faith, and with a better understanding.

Table of Contents

1	TAME THE TONGUE BY PRACTICE	1
2	PRACTICE, BECOMES HABIT, BECOMES LAWS	7
3	PRACTICE, ACTING BECOMES HABIT, BECOMES LAW	11
4	PRACTICE, ACTING BECOMES HABIT, BECOMES LAW	15
5	PRACTICE, BECOMES HABITS, BECOMES LAWS	21
6	PRACTICE, BECOMES HABIT, BECOMES LAW	25
7	TREASURES OF FAITH	31
8	THE TREASURE OF A MAN'S HEART	35
9	THE TRUE VALUE OF THINGS	37
10	PRACTICE, BECOME HABITS, BECOME LAWS	41

1
TAME THE TONGUE BY PRACTICE

"For in many things we all offend. If any man offends not in word, the same is a perfect man and able also to bridle the whole body..."

James 3:2

A perfect man who is able to control his mouth will control his life. Before he controls his life, that person must first learn the words that are life-giving and a blessing. We need to learn how to separate words that will bless, and words that will curse ourselves, as well as others — words that keep us separated from the Father's will. Sinful words hurt and cause pain. Coming and going, a perfect person is one who has the shield of faith, who is the truth of the Word of God that protects His spirit. He is not offended by the words or the action of sinful words. They don't offend or hurt their spirit with words that cause depression or mental illness. Sinful words are our enemy! We need to pay close attention and learn about them.

Let's talk about practicing to learn; you will have to search the wisdom treasures of your heart to be able to come into agreement with me that everything has to be learned by practice through acting. Think about that for a moment! When "Jesus said to learn what that meant," learning requires going over and searching to get a good understanding (*Matt. 9:13*). Anything you are willing to practice with all your heart to achieve, will become your treasure because it's something you truly want and value.

Practice Acting, Becomes Habit, Becomes Law

One of the things I have come to understand is that, once born again, one is like a newborn baby in Christ, like a baby that needs to be taught; to learn by practicing is the mink of the word. Remember that scripture that talks about running the race *(1 Cor. 9:24):* "Everything that goes into running a race, before running there must be practiced." *(Heb. 12:1, Ps. 19:5).* Training to wind, war, and fight learning by practicing, going over and over it until it becomes a habit that is well-learned.

Think about it: A drug habit, an alcohol habit, a habit of thinking, and doing the wrong thing. It's not easy to break an old habit and learn a new habit, uprooting the roots of old habits of the flesh. Under the laws of sin, we unconsciously do things without realizing the danger of what we were doing **(Prov. 22:6).** *Again,* training, preparing for a race by practicing and rehearsing, this is a lifelong practice. Think about a baby: what are some of the things that are needed to teach and train a baby or a child to follow instructions, to trust, to build strong habits by practice? How do you teach them to be humble and giving, to love by giving and sharing?

A person with a good practice habit will always be the best, or better at it. Work on one or two habits at a time and always give yourself something to practice, and based on how they do, you can increase them. In *Matthew 25:15,* we see servants working, practicing to be better than they were, and to do that takes practice. Faith without works.*(James 2:14-17).* It's like when we were in school: to go to the next grade, you had to practice and rehearse to be ready to go to the next level; you also need to practice to become an adult. The tree of the knowledge of good and evil (*Gen. 2:9).* There is no life of understanding when we walk by the ways of the old sinful flesh. *Roman 8:1* says, "Put to practice what you have learned, that is the work. Faith without work produces nothing." Ever learning but never coming to an understanding, and understanding comes from spending time, to understand by meditation (2 **Tim. 3:7).** Practice by putting words to the test. Do they work? Do you need courage? What about boldness, focusing on love and trust, to be better at giving? In mapping out your day and your week, what word or words are you using? We can't do anything without words. *2 Timothy 3:61 says,* "Behold, we put bits in the mouth of the horse." *James 3:3* Words of life are treasures, and words of death are also treasure to some. The words of the thief come to kill, steal, and destroy.

Do you take pleasure in saying words that hurt, words that destroy the emotional state of happiness that a person is in? "Today is the day the Lord has made; I will rejoice and be glad." As I practice acting out His words of life on friends and family, speaking words of love to my neighbor. What word are you going to practice today, this week, or this month, building the character of your house? *(Luke 6:48)*. This is for you and those who would take part in the celebration of what the Lord has done. This is the spirit of the born-again person who is learning about the kingdom, not the "old man." Become emotional and excited about your new self and the progress you are making in your new walk. Become in love with your new self in Christ Jesus. Don't confuse the "new man" in Christ Jesus with the old man of sin. The old spirit man is dead; treat the knowledge from him as dead knowledge. Your new life in Christ Jesus is about educating your new spirit about the things of the Word of God. Your life is made up of spiritual words, live or dead. You become the words that you choose. Nothing is impossible with God, and there is nothing impossible with God's Word in you!

Practice being friends: We never established a friendship relationship with your brother and sister in Christ in a marriage. Marriage in the spirit to Christ Jesus is not the same as a marriage of this world to the flesh. What do I mean? We are the Lord's bride in the spirit, and in the spirit, we are no longer physical husband and wife, but brothers and sisters in Christ Jesus's spiritual marriage. We are learning how to be friends, read books, and get teaching; seek and search for the treasures of understanding in friendship. Everything goes back to your acting; you were created to act. Practice acting to build a strong habit of being friendly. If we think about a child, children normally are loving and giving. Jesus said to become a child, and to truly understand what a child is like, you will have to read about them and ask questions that require seeking. You don't normally see anger, jealousy, or hateful unforgiveness in young children. The reason for that is that there is no understanding of the words they are hearing. If we do some in-depth study on what Jesus meant, "to become like a child," (*Matt. 18:3*) would you say obedience and humility are birth characteristics of a child? What about sharing? Is it impossible to be a child in the adult body of sin? Humble yourself as a child; *Proverbs 22:6 says, "Train up a child in the way he should go, and when he is old he will not depart from it."* Let's put these two verses together. "Train up a child and become as a child;" in this way, you can establish discipline. (The dictionary meaning is the practice of training people to obey rules or a code of behavior.) "But all things are possible with God." All things are possible with us when we believe God's Word. Important piece of information: God doesn't use words that He doesn't mean! When we are seeing the Word of God through the eyes of our flesh, we can't take it seriously. How can two walk live together unless they can come to an agreement or believe the same? This is a hard saying: When one is walking more in the flesh than the other, to put to practice these things will take work. Remind yourself in the spirit that all things are possible to him who believes. Respect is one, listening is another; don't think negatively of the born-again spirit that is living in that body. Be sensitive and try to be more understanding. True love and friends can't be separated; a friendship relationship is built on respect, where trust and reliability are established and nourished on the milk of love *(Deut. 13:6)*. The scripture in *John 15:13* reads, "No greater true love and friends one that lay down their lives for each other's 'sacrifice.'" *Galatians 5:13 says*, "To sow the seed of the word. Boldness *Courageous, confident, and fearless; ready to take risks."*

Think about it way: spiritual words of death are our enemy, not a physical person; when it comes to being bold or courageous, they will be words that you have to fight with and stand against. When words of doubt stand up to stop you from what you are trying to believe, humility, and pride. Even in a physical battle, the other person is going through the same thinking; it's the words that he has to add up into the sentence, that he will follow through for success or failure, and that he must fight the enemy of words of doubt to stay on course. "Dictionary" *Showing or requiring courage conservative, cool, courteous, or cowardly, faint-hearted, fearful, meek, modest, polite, retiring, shy, tactful, timid, timorous dull, ordinary, pale, soft, unimaginative.*

A bold plan is that fear has got to be removed; you have to build up enough strength by practicing acting out those words of faith. You got to rehearse, and how do you rehearse for a play or to be in a wedding? You practice by rehearsing and acting out. In the military, all is about rehearing acting by practice to build a habit. We don't think about rehearsing by practice, to build a habit, we only think about it when it comes to movies. But in reality, if you think about it? We are practicing rehearsing every day, We are making a movie about our life before God and man every day. "Dictionary" means a person whose profession is acting on the stage, in a movie, or on television. Remember the Holy Ghost is an instructor. A person who teaches something: "A driving instructor". The eternal life of the Spirit of God lives in and over everything He has created. Once we began to walk in the life of the spirit, This is something to look into, If you are basing your foundational belief on fear, pride, stubbornness, and lack of humility you will fail. If you study these words, you will see where you will end up. Those who are walking in the knowledge of the old nature can't please God and God can't please them (*Heb. 11:6* and Rom. 8:8). To understand the importance of using and keeping our words, we are nothing and can do nothing without words that add life. We really have to take on the mindset of a child! As newborn babies in Christ Jesus, you may see yourself as a child, think, and act as a child. but you will behave and believe as an adult.

2
Practice, Becomes Habit, Becomes Laws

Time to practice your acting out words: The Lord spoke a word to me months ago about learning to purposely practice acting. Think of *acting* as your work in this body, and purposely say words. Remember the scenes in the movie, *Karate Kid*? Our role in this movie of Christ is to *act* like Christ in everything we do, acting like actors do when making a movie. We are meant to practice building our new nature, like a loving, kind, spiritual person. Have you noticed that you are always practicing? Our focus is to become better at life, better at living. The moment you were born into this world, many of us were not focused on this, but everything had to be learned by practicing acting and building strong, unwavering habits, (*Prov. 22:6*) discovering new ways by continually practicing to be better, and dudging this world and our bodies according to the Bible standard. We are never perfect at anything (*James 3:2*).

There are so many ways to learn to be perfect in speaking words of love to others, as well as to ourselves. When we speak words of love to ourselves, we are loving ourselves; we are ministering to our spirit, God's Word of love. To become better at it, we need to focus our attention on our practice of acting. You are an actor. It's your work; when you go to work, regardless of how you feel, you perform your duties, and act out your acting role on that job. In saying good morning or obeying, even when listening, all has to do with the practice of acting. The tree or the body of this world of good and evil words: Remember, the tree has knowledge of good and evil; we focus on the good, and not the evil, and the good ways of religion, doubt, and the unbelief of our flesh. To think that we have arrived so we can stop focusing on becoming better? The world approves, except for what they consider good *(Matt. 15:2, Matt. 15:20)*. Be better at loving ourselves and others; anytime knowledge of truth comes across our path, we should embrace it, cherish it, and install it into our heart, the place where all of our treasure is kept. To love yourself, is to love God. *Matthew 12:35 says, "A good man out of the good **treasure** of the heart bringeth forth good things; and an evil man out of the evil **treasure** bringeth forth evil things."*

How do you make something valuable to you? You need to take time to gather all the information you have received from the Word of God and decide what is valuable and important. To be carnal-minded, to think like the world, in the old nature, and to believe like the world, is death. This is your valuable treasure as a Christian. We should be in a continual state of mind to learn and to grow, and this comes by practice. If you are walking in and still believe in who you were as the old man, you have not put on Christ in your new nature.

Again, once the knowledge of the truth comes, it will deliver you from the enslavement of the knowledge of sin. This new spiritual baby and child that you are entrusted to teach, to train, are gifted to read, study, and search out the deeper truths of God's Word. The truth comes to set you free; it will take ongoing practice acting to make this a part of your belief. You are an actor. *James 2:20 says, "But wilt thou know, O vain man, that **faith without works** is dead?"* You must keep your focus on being better by practicing. Inventory and guard your new habit. Believe and trust; God can't work in our lives without trust. *Romans 10:10 states, "For with the heart, man **believe**th unto righteousness, and with the mouth, confession is made unto salvation."* Hebrews 11:6 reads, *"**To trust: to rescue from harm, danger, or loss:**"* "A double-minded person has not come to trust," *reads James 1:6*. Do you know how you got where you are and what you will have to do differently? Let me share something with you about living in a world that is run by spiritual forces. If you are walking in the flesh, the old nature, you can't see or understand what is going on in the spirit where God is. Example: Israel walked *(Numb. 32:13). Deuteronomy29:5* indicates that their clothing didn't get old for forty years; do you think they noticed it?

You are the governor, the policeman of your life. You have to make the laws for your protection from God's Word, and enforce those laws in and around your life. After you have put laws in place, now you must protect them by changing your habits and lifestyles. All the laws of life are branches of the Ten Commandments. Keep this in mind that to change your law is to change your habits. We want what others have achieved, but don't want to do what they did to get what they have. *Matthew 7:13-14 says, "Enter ye in at the strait gate."* The straight gate, not the wide and broad way, is one of the reasons for so many not being able to find the treasure of life on the narrow road. "Seek and you will find." The effort it takes to keep standing and seeking to find the treasures of life: **THE TREASURE OF LIFE THAT IS IN GOD'S WORD.** When looking for treasure such as gold, or anything of value, once you have found one, you continually look because there must be more. Then you find another, and another, and you don't stop looking. This is what it is like to find the most valuable treasure of life in God's Word. *John 1:4 says, "In Him was **life**, and that **life** was the Light of men." (John 3:16, John 3:36, John 4:14, John 6:33.) John 1:4 says, "In Him was **life**, and that **life** was the Light of men." John 14:6 states that, "Jesus said unto him, 'I am the Way, the Truth, and the **Life**; no man cometh unto the Father, but by Me.'"*

These scriptures tell us of the value of the words of Jesus. *John 6:63 says, "It is the **Spirit** that quickeneth; the flesh profiteth nothing. The **words** that I speak unto you, they are **spirit**, and they are life."* Think about acting, and all that goes into acting. The dictionary definition lists: *"**1.** A person who behaves in the manner of a character, usually by reciting scripted dialogue, in order to entertain an audience, especially in a play, movie, or television show."*

We imitate and act like our Father God. *Matthew 5:48 says, "Be ye therefore perfect, even as your Father who is in Heaven is perfect."* We were created to act like we do it all the time; we don't see it as that. We practice "learn-acting," and act out what is given to us. Nothing is done without first practicing acting; take a word you must learn as you act on it; take this scripture: *Matthew 7:24 "Therefore, whosoever heareth these sayings of Mine and doeth them, I will liken him unto a wise man, who built his house upon a rock."* Matthew. 18:4 suggests that the love of God has to be practiced, and we must stop practicing the love of this world "every day." Put your focus on a word, learn that word, and act it out; what are the characteristics of a "humble person." Think about this seriously. Everything we do in this life is practicing to be better, focus or not. Put your mind on what you are doing. Unless it is a quality decision, your decision will not stand for anything. "Believe" you are to know, trust, and rely on; what you believe all starts with a word, and the understanding of a word or words.

What am I practicing today that I should not or should be practicing? Remember, all practice, in the beginning, is painful — both spiritual and physical. "Think" about what I just said: spiritual pain. It's the *spiritual* pain that stops us from walking in God's Word, give up and quit. Prepare for the spiritual pain; like all pain, it comes from working out. In the beginning, it's hard, but as you continue it gets better and easier. In anything that we are attempting to do for the first time, there will be pain; think about sports, the military, and Christians in their walk in love. Pain doesn't mean quitting or giving up; it means keep going until it stops. It will take *hard* spiritual work; how many of us have given up because of the pain of the fight? Let's take a spiritual look at these words: "hard work for spiritual and physical gain."

3
Practice Acting Becomes Habit, Becomes Law

It's the laws of habits that cause you to become strong or weak at anything, and laws are established by *words*. Words, true or false, become habits, and habits become laws from practicing *(Rom. 8:2)*. Everything begins or starts like this. If you want changes in your life, start the practice of acting and doing the thing you want to do, or making a new habit. Our job in the Body of Christ is to rebuild or to build new habits by practicing acting, until we become the best at walking in the spirit of love. *"Practice putting My Word in your heart so it will become a habit to serve My Word."* We are learning and studying to be improved unto God *(2 Tim. 2:15)*. These two laws of life and death are at war with our members, the law of sin and death, sinful words, words of life, the habits of sin and death. These are habits of not involving God in our every day-to-day walk in this life. *Isaiah 26:3 says, "Thou wilt keep him in* **perfect peace,**... *In all your ways acknowledge Me, think of me, make me part of your conversation, your decision."* **Deuteronomy 28:1-14, 2 states:**

> *and all these blessings shall come on thee and overtake thee,... I say that you will be blessed going out and coming,* "Are you sending me out before you? Are you acknowledging me in you? Are you in conversation with Me today? I am wiser, stronger than you. I know more about this life than

> *you, I know what will happen today and tomorrow before it happens, do you think you can trust me?*

"Depression" is an insult that can be a spiritual pain, disrespect, or is the pain of loving when there is no appreciation. The weak will feel pain when it comes to suffering; walk in faith. *Romans 15 says, "We then that are strong ought to bear the infirmities of the weak..."* **1 Timothy 6:12** *reads, "Fight the good fight of faith. Lay hold on eternal life, whereunto thou art also called and hast professed a good profession before many witnesses."* **Romans 14:21** discusses spiritual pain, your focus. Rejoice and reward yourself with words of encouraging love. Until those words are removed from your heart, you can't go forward. Fight the old failure of the old nature, the old identity of the flesh. Your emotions are controlled by words you believe are going to set you free, being excited about doing something good. Put on the "new you." Anyone who comes to Christ Jesus has enough sense of awareness that the old life was a failure. Love yourself for what you have achieved, and have confidence in this new you that is being created by the Word of God. **Philippians 3:13** discusses forgetting those things, the old ways. Have you ever acted out words that add up to a sentence with your male or female friend? If we think about it, everything has to be rehearsed in our minds, then acted out. Husbands and wives act like they are on a date for the first time they just met, on their best behavior, with your well dress personality with all the trimming. Go back to those days. Bring the spirit of God's love into what you plan to do. Going on a date with someone requires a lot of acting, the normal way of acting. What happened over the days, months, and years when we stop practicing and acting those words?

Think about the word "forgetting," and take yourself into the spirit of forgetfulness; even this can be practiced **Philippians 3:13** discusses the spiritual power to forget. "Let no man deceive himself," **says** *1 Corinthians 3:18.*

To decide your time, your decision about the pleasure you want to enjoy. You are free to choose now that you are in Christ Jesus. Practice preparing your day of pleasure the week or month before. Live in the spiritual pleasure of the joy of happiness. Before and after a special day, or the holidays, how excited are you about it being the pleasure of that day? It fills your heart with joy. In His presence, there is a joy to the fullest; in the presence of His Word, there is joy when His Word is in you, and your mind is on His Word.

I use this illustration about learning to ride a bicycle and all the things that can be done; as you pursue your discovery of increasing knowledge that the Father invested in riding a bicycle. Everything is this way "Discovery" You discover as you practice; think about it in terms of walking in the spirit, and in the love of God, remember this verse: "Faith without works is dead." I think about lowing my blood pressure as I pursue ways of lowing my pressure I discover new ways of doing things to lower it. What many of us are doing including me at times we run to the doctor; after the doctor tells you what you must do, go and discover ways of doing it without the meds. Once born again, we come into the knowledge of the truth of words of the spirit; the world associates pain with the physical, not the spiritual. Depression is spiritual pain that is connected to anger, sadness, offense, and the loss of a loved one; these feelings are spiritual. As believers, this is our fight, our war in the spirit. ***2 Corinthians 10:3*** states, *"For though we walk in the flesh, we do not war according to the flesh." **1 Peter 2:11** says, "Dearly beloved, I beseech you as strangers and pilgrims, abstain from fleshly lusts which war against the soul."* The only way to overcome and defeat the pain of sin is to fight with God's Word; stop running from the pain of sinful words, and destroy them with God's Word. Remember that the verse "Faith without works or practice is dead," has power. ***Romans 6:14*** says, *"For sin shall not have dominion over you, for ye are not under the law, but under grace."* Pain is to deter your thinking and the pursuit of your dreams; you must fight back with the most powerful force in existence: God's Word of love. Once your words become a habit by rehearsing and practicing, they become law and your prayer will be heard. This is why we are commanded to speak His Word.

4
Practice Acting Becomes Habit, Becomes Law

Luke 1:14 *tells you that* because you are acknowledging Him, His Word in all you do, now you are in His presence. What makes this all fulfilling is when you can be in agreement about it. Continually acting every day, always practice, rehearse, and act until it becomes a habit. Only born-again spirits, with the help of God's Word, can continually practice the love of Christ Jesus until it becomes law.

Practice by rehearing to be better; life is this way, and everything must be rehearsed. Remember that words of life are alive; even movie actors use them, and they receive their reward of pleasure, evil or good. God didn't create anything with simple-mindedness. Let's look at the laws of driving: we have been practicing them for so long that we do them naturally. We choose to obey them. What about the laws of God's Word that you have not been taught? You will discover more as you practice if you are failing in any area of your life. It's because of a law you are not obeying or practicing. Remember that *every* word is a law, and unless you look them up and study them, how will you know what to do? Practice learning to obey laws out of your new nature. The struggle that is in breaking an unwanted, no-good, unproductive habit is destroying the good fruits of your life. All habits are created out of our desire for pleasure; put this into the treasure of your heart. We are creative beings and everything involves creating; we take words, and create from them, then words become laws. Let's get one thing straight: how important are words or a word? Take some time to go over this, and how do you decide what word, and its value, to put into the treasure of your heart, and to add to the completion of the puzzle of your life? We don't get a true, pure understanding of the meat of a word or words, unless we meditate and bring in a harvest from the word.

Remember I said that everything begins with practice. Practice becomes a habit, and habit becomes law. These are the steps to change: To become better, stronger, and wiser, all starts with practice; we don't think about it in this way when we are walking carnal-minded, like the world. We are practicing and acting all the time, practicing being the same. We are better at doing nothing, or better at improving our lives as Christians. Words have spiritual weight because they are heavy or light. We can be overwhelmed by the burdens and the weight of them; it takes continual practice lifting and carrying them to be spiritually strong. The scripture that comes to mind. the men he gave talent. "I have meat to eat you no not..." says *John 4:34*.

Putting the Word to work by practice, they got better and were rewarded with more faith and works. Practice putting spiritual words to work to be a better child of God. Let's overlook the lies and setbacks of our fleshly bodies, and enjoy who we are spiritually; let's fall in love with the words from the Bible that create our character. Appreciate the kind of person you become and don't think about going back to the old ways of the flesh; take pleasure in who you are, and talk to yourself about how much you love yourself by loving the words that make you a better person. The quality of the person you become depends on the word you value your treasure because God loves you. What about using the authority of God's Word over the way you eat, putting into practice a different way of eating? Practice resisting the old ways of sin, using your shield of faith against becoming angry. When sinful words are used toward you, you have to practice acting being a stronger person in the Lord. Think of ways and things to practice. What about anger? We all need to practice managing the word "anger." "Be angry and sin not." We were given the authority as believers to control words, and *all* words; taking control of your words is taking control of the words you choose. *Proverbs 18:21 says, "Death and life are in the power of the tongue, and they that love it shall eat the fruit thereof."* *Ephesians 4:26* suggests it becomes a habit to practice fasting once or twice a week.

Live a life of fasting by controlling your portions. Let's go back to what I said earlier. Once practice becomes a *habit*, the habit becomes *law*; then, you do it naturally. Remember the Holy Ghost and ask Him to help you with your decisions and scheduling (*John 14:26*). This is your week or month to focus; we get better by practice, and get a little stronger each day. Take pleasure in who you are becoming: this includes the fruits of the Spirit; practice being loving, polite, and kind to yourself in a hostile, angry atmosphere. Always speak loving, encouraging words to yourself, regardless of your mistakes. The way the Lord has it when you love others with "His" love of His Word, you love yourself at the same time. Keep in mind you are destroying the old habit, the works of the "old man" of the flesh. Ask yourself day to day, moment by moment, what am I practicing — the Word of God or the work of the flesh? Once you make up your mind with the help of the Lord to make a new habit of God's Word in your life, you will enjoy the new you. Practice showing and being loving, while resisting sinful anger. God's Word works, and once we put it to work, we give God's Word something to do. Think of it this way: what goes in you comes out of you. Don't let sinful words take dominion over the love of God in your heart. "The joy of loving is your strength." Wives and husbands, you are actors. Are you practicing acting what it takes to be a godly mate? Taking words every day to act kind, polite, and extra sweet is a gift of love to you and the Lord Jesus.

From the Bible manual: this is your new identity. Speak to yourself about who you are, and take a look in the book of James 1:25 so you don't forget who you are. By looking into the perfect laws of the Word of God in Bible study and fellowshipping. Say good things to yourself every day, and make it your day to practice acting good, loving, and kind things for yourself. If you are more fleshly-minded, you will not be willing to practice God's ways of love. Once or twice a week decide on a love play; remember, you are acting, then it's time to rehearse a lot of feeling that goes into this play. You will discover new ways and new plays, and live a life of plays. Start with saying words of love, and take time out for this. The Bible tells us the meaning of the word of the law that is controlling this world "think" about it for a moment. What words or laws are governing this planet when it comes to what God's Word says about it? We see the evil that is in existence here on earth; words are backed up by their actions Words are true, and words tell us the meaning of a thing. The words "murder" or "kill": what are the meanings of these words? "To take a life;" without a dictionary, what good are words or books? We, as believers, shouldn't be deceived by the lies of the devil of this world; remember Eve and the conversation she had with the devil in the serpent? The word was "to die or not;" she didn't go to the dictionary of the Tree of Life that was in the Garden of Eden. He accepted without researching the truth of the words of the devil; we, as believers, are acting like our first Mother Eve. Don't judge or make a decision without a thorough investigation of the meaning of a word or words.

Talk to yourself. Make up plays about you, with you in it. You alone acted out, rehearsing to yourself; "example how do we act toward the Lord." *Ephesians 5:19 says, "Speaking to one another in psalms and hymns and spiritual songs, singing and making melody in your heart to the Lord. Read the testimonies of my faithfulness to those that learn to trust the words that are written about me. The choice is yours; practice believing."* **2 Chronicles 7:14** states, *"You need to learn about me, learn my ways, the way I do things says the Lord."* John 4:24 reads:

> *I am a Spirit. I do things in the Spirit, that is where I live, now you are my child born of my Spirit you need to learn how to walk in the spirit where I am. My word has the power to heal the sick, there is a difference between my words of life and the words of death, you can't confuse the two, you can't speak blessing out of one part of your mouth and cursing out of the other part of your mouth. You must clean out your heart of doubt, fear, unbelief, unforgiveness; curse words that keep you from my blessing. For example, walking in my word of love in fellowship one with the other. It's imposable to walk in the spirit without focus everything require focus.*

Isaiah 26:3 says, "Thou wilt keep him in perfect peace, whose mind is stayed on Thee, because he trusteth in Thee." James 1:7 says, "A <u>double</u>-minded person for let, not that man think that he shall receive anything of the Lord." Numbers 23:19 states, "God is **not** a man, that He should **lie**; neither the son of man, that He should repent. Hath He said, and shall He **not** do it? Or hath He spoken, and shall He **not** make it good?" "Any time you come to me for anything, you must believe in my word, and you can only believe what is true from the dictionary of life's words. What does the word "ager" look like coming from a person? What does the dictionary say? A lie will be anything that is not in the dictionary. Make it a part of your most precious treasure that is in your heart. I only obey My laws and all of My blessings are laws; all of My gifts are laws that work every time. Once My Word is the treasure of your heart, it becomes a habit, which becomes law. *(Matt. 17:20)* "All of your healing will come this way, remember what I said, speak what you want to happen; as it is with My word that is the treasure of My heart goes out of My mouth inter your heart, it is I that speak, we are one My Word, it's My Word is alive *(Heb. 4:12; Isa. 51:16, Ps. 15:4)* What does it mean to swear to do something, to follow through, and decide to do something, then do it?

5
Practice, Becomes Habits, Becomes Laws

Imitate your Father in Heaven *(John 14:23)*. Putting His Word to practice, making His Word a part of your way of living, the Word that is in your heart, spoken out of your mouth, returns back to Him. Nothing is too hard for the God-Word to do; His healing power is only released when you truly believe in His Word, which is the treasure of your heart. Imitating is to act like your Father. (Eph. 5:1). You have put His Word to practice, know they work. Now, His Word has become law to you, rooted, with strong habits. Who are you? I am in Christ Jesus, and one with Him; He is in me and I am in Him. His Spirit and His Word have made us one. Life is about the practice of making strong habits to be good at everything.

Once the habit becomes law, then the law takes over. The love for what you decided to do, the pleasure of it, and the joy of it, all come within the law of the habit. Once you get there or start doing it you fall in love with it and value it. How did God create things? From the words of His mouth and His heart. It's not the Word of God in the mouth of your old nature; those words come out of the mouth of that man who has no power to free you. Those words are tied into your sinful feeling that controls your emotion. Once the Word of God becomes the treasure of your heart, your emotion flows with His Word. Depression, anger, anxiety, the difficulties you have of accepting the death of a loved one, unforgiveness, the power to love yourself with God's Word, and to receive God's love; only the living Word of God can set us free. I want to share something about loving yourself, and how words affect us inward and outwardly. Words that hurt cause pain to the person who receives them. Those words of sin hurt you as well, because they were received at one time. Every time you fail at something, you feel depressed and angered; you feel like ending it, giving up on your dreams. This is the old man, the flesh. The new man who is born of God's Spirit never feels this way because God's Spirit is his helper. If you see yourself as a new person in Christ Jesus, you will appreciate how much you have grown and gotten better, stronger, and wiser. But, if your focus is on the old you, it's too much to overcome and you give up. We have a helper in The Holy Ghost to see ourselves as newborn babies in Christ, not as an older person in this body of sin.

Again, practice loving yourself with God's Word. If you need confidence about what you want to do, find Scripture, and sow them into your heart by saying who you are. Live by every Word (*Matt. 4:4*). Think about this. If God says His Word never fails, then what have you been saying about yourself? We live by the power of words; we know, by life itself, words work. These scriptures are worth repeating: *Isaiah 55:11; Isaiah 51:1615* [16] "And I have put *My words in thy mouth...*" Deuteronomy 30:19 says, "*I call heaven and earth to record this day against you that I have set before you life and death, blessing and cursing. Therefore choose life, that both thou and thy seed may live.*"

Choose the words of life that will set you free from the words that make you a slave; to sin that cause you to be under the curse and not under the blessing. Again everything spiritually and physically needs to be practiced to become a habit, this is where I believe we as Christians miss it. We must be willing to put in the work; the Holy Ghost is not going to do the things *we* should be doing. "For example, you are having problems in your home and in your personal life, you are praying for God to move and bring peace. It will not come until we use God-Word, God does all of His work through His people from His Word." Look at the healings and the miracles that happen: all were done by His people. When praying, ask the Holy Ghost, "What must I do?" The problems we have in our marriages, we need to walk them through God's love by practice, not the way one loves in this world. When we choose not to serve the Lord by obeying His Word, then we stop the ongoing ministry of Jesus. "People" began to put into practice the fruits of God's love (*Gal. 5:22-23*). What fruits are you bearing on your tree? For this New Year's resolution, purposely focus on a fruit or fruits. Get about bearing fruits, so others can come and eat the fruits of your tree; our testimony should be about the fruit or fruits that are working in our lives.

Remember, the farmer planted seeds into the ground to reap a harvest? The seed, being in baby form, takes time to grow. *Hebrews 5:13 says, "For every one that useth milk is unskilled in the word of righteousness, for he is a babe."* Like a baby who is practicing to crawl, then walk, we, as babies, need to humble our flesh unto God our Father. Are you practicing the word "servant?" Are you making it a part of the treasure of your heart? All these things will take time, but don't be discouraged and give up *(Eph. 6:14)*. Every day, every month, every year, our focus is on fruits. *Revelation 22:2 says, "In the midst of the street of it, and on either side of the river, there was the Tree of Life, which bore twelve kinds of fruit and yielded her fruit every month; and the leaves of the tree were for the healing of the nations."*

This is a love tree and the fruits it bore are kindness, being polite, and patience, Look at the word leaves of the trees, they were for healing, Can we apply this verse today? Love itself heals. Practice developing a stronger habit of being patient, and kind while driving; when you are cursing at everybody and everything remember you are practicing to bear fruits. Focus on your thinking, and start the day out with this focus there will be a battle going on in your mind to stay on track. With the way you want to think, mentally you are fighting to keep your mind fixed on what you have decided to practice. *Psalm 141:4 says, "Incline not my heart to any evil thing, to practice wicked works.."*. Micah 2:1 suggests practicing, rehearsing in your mind again, and the more you practice, you discover new ways of doing. Child of God, if you are carnal-minded, fleshly-minded, then the body rules, and this applies to you. *1 Samuel 23:9 says, "And David knew that Saul secretly practiced mischief against him…"* Jealousy. *Romans 8:5 reads, "For those who are according to the flesh mind the things of the flesh."* And you are deceived by your emotions and feelings. We make our decision about loving and accepting someone based on the good emotional feelings that we have created. That was created from the tree of the knowledge of good and evil. Think about it: loving someone is based on our emotional feelings, and the knowledge we received from the world; how emotional we can be about them, and the way we think about them. Words that are true; must be proven that they work, and they give lifelong results. Before you can become emotional about them. You must do intense study, searching for truth. Everything is about valuable investment into the life of our newborn spirit; as newborn babies, in Christ Jesus, we will suffer with Him.

The teaching of the old nature thinks it foolish to suffer for doing the right thing *(John 6:63)*. "Humility." Our proof is from watching television programs and listening to others, never taking the time to make sure that they are truly words spoken that have been investigated, And that the fruits of the Spirit are rooted in what is said. We are never hurt by the words or the action of another person, you have deceived your heart with unproven words you decided to believe without investigation. There is protection in forgiveness; there is protection in the truth *(John 8:32)*. The question that should be asked is: what about the fruits of the Spirit? Are they talking about them? It takes time to see the evidence of fruits once they have been planted and need to be protected. *Galatians 5:22 says, "But the fruit of the Spirit is love..."* We can't take these words for granted.

6
Practice, Becomes Habit, Becomes Law

Understand what God had said comes first, *then* become emotional about it. How much value and respect do you put on your emotions? As of now, our emotions are governed by damaging lies and deception, and we are controlled by them. You see how your emotions were built on the lies of this world; watch out for your emotions when it comes to friends and family loved ones, the old earthly ways of our emotion. By the knowledge of this world and the flesh, we are led into things by our emotions. As you come into a greater understanding of God's Word, your emotions change. Do you know what is in your heart? *Can* you know what is in your heart? I believe you can, to some degree, here on earth. You can know the fruits of love that are in your heart or the fruits of words of sin that still remain in your heart from your old nature. Galatians 6:8 says, *"For he that soweth to his flesh shall of the flesh reap corruption; but he that soweth to the Spirit shall of the Spirit reap life everlasting."*

I think we need to give more focus on how we speak and how we act. It tells us a lot about the ways of our old nature. This scripture is talking about what you have sowed for your spiritual food; you sowed time and work to reap a paycheck. How much time you are putting into studying the Word of God? Back to practicing, rehearsing, and acting. You will never be as good as the person who practices. It takes life-long practice to live a prosperous life, so what are you practicing?

Run the race. Again, are you practicing how to be more polite in your ways of speaking? Are you practicing controlling words of anger? What about the fruits of the Spirit? Practice makes you better at whatever you are going after, so practice to be the best at being considerate to others. Your words will develop into a habit that becomes law, and the law causes you to become all that you want to be. It's hard work at the beginning, like all things when you are out of shape. Do a little at a time. Your words spoken have to go before your acting; what do I mean? Remember, God created everything with His words, words released in the atmosphere of the Spirit. What did Jesus say about the mountain? Matthew 21:21 says, *"Out of the heart, the mouth speaks. Whatever you bind on earth with the words of your mouth."* Say what you are going to do over and over first, early in the morning, in the daytime, and at night! Your words will be the hard work; speaking them out is the spiritual work, the spiritual warfare that you will have to "focus" on. Put things in your heart so that, "out of the treasures of the heart, the mouth speaks." Whatever you bind on earth with the words of your mouth…"

Say what you are going to do first over and over, early in the morning, in the daytime, and at night! Your words will be the hard work; speaking them out is the spiritual work, the spiritual warfare that you will have to "focus" on. Putting things in your heart, "out of the treasures of the heart the mouth speaks." Once you speak a word over and over it becomes law and we are controlled by the words of our mouth, so begin to replace the old words that once controlled your lives in the flesh. Begin to recognize God's Word to have full authority in your life. Stop saying I can't, now it's what God says about what I can do in Him. Put on Christ, live out Christ, and speak the words that you have chosen for your new identity. Because everything must be created from the word or words we receive and believe. The people of the world, the flesh, believe in what they see: the evidence, the truth about anything is what can be proven from it in a court of law, proof of what you believe to be true *(1 Peter 3:15)*. We must make this saying a part of our treasure, "important" to bear any kind of fruit. You must approach, and go after it, to bring it to pass. Like a baby, every new idea and new belief, though, comes to us in baby form: milk of the Word, not meat. They need to be practiced to develop an ongoing habit.

If we approach these fruit verses with a carnal, fleshly mind, we become like the world. Think about these scriptures: *1 Corinthians 1:21,27 and Romans 8:7.* To be spiritually minded, the first thought is, I am a baby that needs to learn how to be a mature Christian. This I believe is the deception part of our understanding, of our growth, because we don't understand our old nature, we don't follow through; the difficulties we are having from our old nature it is not a baby. We divert back to our old nature when we don't have the understanding; there is an earthly understanding, our own understanding not a godly understanding. *Proverbs 3:5-6 says, "Trust in the Lord with all thine heart, and lean not unto thine own understanding; in all thy ways acknowledge Him, and He shall direct thy paths," (Matt. 18:3,4; Mark 10:15).* The old nature, the teaching of the flesh, is not you, the born-again spirit man; the teaching of the old nature is to criticize, speak less of, tear down. "To the unclean, everything is unclean," *Romans 14:14* says. When you hear words like that, it's from the old nature. Let's go back to everything that has to be learned. I went to a funeral service where I had to speak; I had to fight to be comfortable and not nervous. And the Lord's brought back to my remembrance that everything has to be practiced even this; I didn't think about practicing in this way. What about learning to walk in the love of God against the old nature? *Romans 8:5 says, "For those who are according to the flesh mind the things of the flesh; but those who are according to the Spirit, the things of the Spirit."* "Think about" everyone must experience pain and suffering to learn anything in this life. Whatever you want to do in this life; pain and suffering come with it until you learn how to. Again, it's like learning to ride a bicycle for the first time. Many, because of the rejection and disappointment they face while trying to minister, turn and quit; put this as a treasure in your heart that learning everything must be approached like a baby on milk.

"Practice." You will make mistakes; it's part of the process. It's like playing a sport in front of a crowd for the first time. Even words all have to be learned and put into practice to build a habit; think about it how much time do we spin learning a word, by practicing how to use them? Learning to use words is like learning to ride a bicycle, ride a horse, or drive a car; words are more important because they are used to explain everything. Trust, faithfulness, obedience, loyal, politeness, consideration, respectful; how much do we know about these words? It was passed down from the beginning, the man got his information from the street, words of the devil; he didn't go to the dictionary of the tree of life before receiving, and believing words out of the mouth of unlearned men. Before there was a Bible, there was a dictionary. It's no longer that I am a drug addict or an alcoholic, it's only bad habits. Change the habit of the old nature; it's like a baby that has a habit of sucking its finger, Change the habit and you will stop the addiction. Stop looking at it from the sinful, physical viewpoint, and see it as a habit. The two words mean the same, but how you view them is the effect they will have on you.

In search of a mate, how are we going to know the person? What are the characteristics of a good mate, and how would you recognize them? What are the habits of that person that take time if you know what you are looking for. Look at the word and find it in this verse: *Proverbs 18:22 says, "Whosoever findeth a wife findeth a good thing and obtaineth the favor of the Lord."*

Here, he is not talking about a physical person, it's words that tell us what to look for in a person of value and respect, and the Lord is leading and guiding their life. You can't find the person until you find the knowledge that keeps you in agreement. Remember, the Bible talks about the treasure of a man's heart; his treasure is what he believes and understands, and what he believes in will be what is acted out in their life. Again, the scripture talks about you will know them by their fruits. *"Those who are according to the Spirit, the things of the Spirit,"* says *Galatians 5: 15*. Everything has to be a research-dictionary for the pure truth when it comes to God's Word. The more understanding you have of a thing-word the stronger your belief will be about it; life itself should teach us the value of the things that add life to our living.

The knowledge of this world that governs us is deceptive, lies like a loss of memory. James 1:23.22 states:

> But be ye doers of the Word and not hearers only, deceiving your own selves. [23] For if any be a hearer of the Word and not a doer, he is like unto a man beholding his natural face in a mirror; [24] for he beholdeth himself, and then goeth his way and straightway forgetteth what manner of man he was. [25] But whoso looketh into the perfect law of liberty and continueth therein, he being not a forgetful hearer but a doer of the work, this man shall be blessed in his deed.

The only time most of us value life are when it is taken from us; then we fight to keep it, but the word of God teaches us to value all the gifts of God to us. The more you invest in what you believe the valuable it becomes; words themselves have life in them, God's Word is alive. John 6:63 You are seeking, searching for the valuable understanding of what the word of God is talking about. I am emotional, and passionate about prayer because I know the value of prayer and that prayer works. I am emotional, and passionate when studying the bible because I know that I learn a lot from reading. There is nothing more important than educating yourself about the Kingdom of heaven, and truth. Husbands and wives rehearse plays and words to say to each other; keep this in your thinking you are building your character by practice. this is our treasure. Remember what was said, "out of a man's heart he speaks words that are good". *Proverb 10:14 says, "Wise men lay up knowledge."* (in the treasure of their heart so He can bring in a harvest of life.

7
TREASURES OF FAITH

The treasures of what is right, the treasures of what you believe about people — right or wrong — is the treasure of what you believe about yourself. Your belief can stabilize you or fail you. Balancing and strengthening your belief about what you believe, all the treasures are in the heart, not your head. A thought or a word will come to your mind; is it a treasure that you believe about yourself, or can help you? If you believe in your feeling, pain, or loving feeling; you should be controlled by words that are right and that you have an understanding of. Think before you decide to believe anything, do research, is your life worth it? What is the value of your life? What are the values of the words of life? What about our natural body? How valuable are the parts of it? Let's look at the dictionary and see what it says about the life of some things: "Growth, reproduction, and adaptation to the environment."

There is nothing more valuable than the life of something; we are here to protect the life that God has gifted us: the life of the parts of the body, the life of the soul, and the life of the spirit. There is a wasted life, destroyed life, and the blood is the life of the body. ***Deuteronomy 30:15,19 says, "I put before you life and good death and evil..."*** A flower or plant, when alive, is beautiful, and lovely to look at. What about a newborn baby or a puppy full of life, excitement, flowing, and bursting with love? Can you remember the days when you were filled with life? What are the things that God has given to us that will keep life flowing in us? Food, water, the air we breathe. What about knowledge and the understanding of knowledge? Would you say that knowledge is also life to us?

Without knowledge, how will we know what we need to do to live and enjoy life to its fullest? **Romans 7:9** says, *"For I was alive apart from the law once, but when the commandment came, sin revived and I died."* But, when he became of age, he died deceived by lies, and those lies got into his heart he believed the lie and he died. Life was removed from him, and he started lying, stealing, and cursing those words that got into his heart. His spirit died like a flower dried up and had no life in it, dead to God and His word. The food for our soul and our spiritual heart is the word of God because God's word is alive, adds life, and restores life. **Romans 6:11** says, *"Likewise reckon ye also yourselves to be dead indeed unto sin, but alive unto God through Jesus Christ our Lord."*

Begin to live a life, full of life, from the mouth of God. Remember the words of Jesus in *John 10:10: "The thief cometh not but to steal and to kill and to destroy. I am come that they might have life and that they might have it more abundantly,"* (*Matt. 6:21* and *2 Cor. 4:7*). Think about the things or words that have value and the ones that don't: Put your mind, and your thinking, on value: what is important, and what is good for you. The value of the life of the body of our marriage. Your natural body needs for food and water. Your spiritual marriageable body needs. Happiness, peace, laughter, thanksgiving, and a blessed home. This is your focus; when you decide to focus your attention on a particular word or a particular subject. That's when those words begin to open themselves up to you, fresh understanding comes, and the truth is revealed; put it to practice, try it and see if you don't get blessed. God's Word is liked to be admired, respected, and you should delight yourself in it. This, I believe, is taking a fruit from the Tree of Life that is God Himself *(Rom. 8:1)*.

Our value comes with our new birth in the spirit; this is why we need to have a better understanding of who we are spiritually. All of this information is in the Bible. You are valuable. What makes you valuable, important, and precious? Out of all of God's creations, there is *none* more valuable than you. Get this into your thinking and down in your heart! The very best of Himself was deposited in us, and our spirit yearned for the pure fruit of God's Word. "Let's make man in our image," Genesis 2 says. The fruits, the wealth of the Holy Spirit, is love; joy is of value because "joy of the Lord is our strength." Do you know that you are responsible for your growth, to teach yourself, and to train yourself in the things of God? Treasures of faith *(Deut. 30:15,19)*

The Bible talks about the treasure of a man's heart: The treasure of God is His Word, and the treasure He is talking about is His words. Words created everything, words are what govern this planet and words govern heaven, words are the life of everything. As we begin to study and understand words, we will have more success in our everyday life. I am thinking about being in a marriage and the words that are spoken, spouses speaking to each other, words of doubt, words that don't motivate but tear down our motivation to prosper in God's Word of love. We need to be around words that minister God's Word to us, encourage us, strengthen us, and cause us to think positively.

We are to speak words of faith and keep the presence of the love of the Lord in our home. What God can do in us and *through* us, and for others. Remember the words of God in *Isaiah 5 -13 13*. Words create peace in a house, again filling the atmosphere of the house with love, and loving words, and there will be the presence of God and His working angels. We are talking about words like "thank you very much," "excuse me," words like "I am sorry," and "I was wrong;" God blessed you. We need to study the Word of God and get an understanding of what is right and wrong. We need to have a love or treasure for what is right and what is wrong. Remember what was said "out of a man's heart he speaks," words that are good. *Proverbs 10:14 says, "Wise men lay up knowledge: but the mouth of the foolish..."* You see what is being talked about: words building up or tearing down, the right decision.

Knowing what is right helps you make the right choices in all things. We have been taught that we can pick and choose when to be right and when to be stubbornly and selfishly, disagreeable; not knowing that we can't pick and choose words of life and words of death. Jesus said something profound in *Matthew 26:41: "Watch and pray, that ye enter not into temptation. The spirit indeed is willing, but the flesh is weak."* We were born and raised by the things of our five senses. All our decisions are from our senses, what we believe what we can see. In the " kingdom," you believe what you understand from words. In the Old Covenant, God use <u>signs</u> so they can believe. <u>Read</u> these verses in *James 3:11*-18. We must respect God and His Word. These are our treasures; these are our treasures of life, so many of us have lost our first love of the commandments (*Mark 4:3*). We begin at the third verse: "*Hearken; Behold, there went out a sower to sow...*" The teacher is talking about words: Words are being spoken to the listener, and the treasures of our hearts take authority over what is being said and needed. But some words are not received right away for different reasons; some receive, but the word had no root, and was not able to get rooted. [5] *And some fell on stony ground...*

I made certain that certain laws are not a part of my life at my home, and words of doubt and unbelief are not spoken out of my mouth in my home. Can we see or understand the difference between the spirit and the flesh? "Think about that." In the spirit, we become one with God and His Word. Words are powerful, and they have God's created existent life in them, but in this world, they must be separated, divided (Gen. 3:1-6). Rightly dividing the Word (2 Tim. 2:15). Your life depends or hinges on dividing, separating words in your life; words are going to cause you to be successful or not.

8
THE TREASURE OF A MAN'S HEART

"But He answered and said unto them, 'An evil and adulterous generation seeketh after a sign, and there shall no sign be given to it, but the sign of the prophet Jonah,'" (Prov. 7:2). "Keep my commandments and live; and my law as the apple of thine eye," (Matthew 6:19). "Lay not up for yourselves treasures upon earth, Remember this verse "out of the heart the mouth speaks." That is why it's by faith not by sight. There is an earthly treasure of belief, an earthly treasure of love, it's not our spiritual value of things of this world. Look at this scripture: *Mark 8:35.* Your life consists of the treasure of your heart! *(Luke 6:45).* The things he is bringing forth out his mouth is controlling his life. In the book of *James 3: 6,* there is no greater treasure on Earth or in Heaven than the treasure of the Word of God. This scripture tells us something about the treasure of words: *Proverb 3: 1-4 says:*

> *My son, forget not my law, but let thine heart keep my commandments; 2 for length of days and long life and peace shall they add to thee. 3 Let not mercy and truth forsake thee; bind them about thy neck, write them upon the tablet of thine heart. 4 So shalt thou find favor and good understanding in the sight of God and man.*

Talking about wisdom words that have been accumulated, that give a true understanding about the righteousness of life *(John 6: 63).* Think of the things that treasure can buy or purchase here on earth. Now, think about what things we can purchase from Heaven with the treasure of the Word of God, taking the treasure-wealth of the word and purchasing blessings. Jesus told the people that came to Him to be able to purchase healing, a sound mind, the blind, and deaf possess an evil spirit, it will cost you something of value. The value of your faith-belief, and understanding of the word, gives life for something of more value. What are we willing to sacrifice, give up of the flesh to get the understanding of God's Word? What we believe is life to us. For the greater treasure: remember both treasures are in the heart. *"A good man out of the good treasure of his heart bringeth forth that which is good; and an evil man out of the evil treasure of his heart bringeth forth that which is evil"* To know what is in your heart by what is coming out of the mouth, and your behavior. *Matthew 13: 44 says, "Again, the Kingdom of Heaven is like unto treasure hid in a field, which, when a man hath found, he hideth; and for the joy thereof goeth and selleth all that he hath, and buyeth that field."*

Again, what are you willing to give up for the treasures of life? We must start valuing life and the things that are life *(John 3:6)*. I use this illustration in many discussions, like riding a bicycle. From a natural standpoint, you cannot tell me or teach me how to ride a bicycle as a child; everything was taught by signs. Follow this, do this, and not by reading, or learning to understand. Remember that everything has to be created by using our imagination. In *John 20:29, "Jesus said unto him, 'Thomas, because thou hast seen Me, thou hast believed....'"* "We are drawing to focus on the outward and not the inward," (Matt. 12:39).

Focus and work to stay focused spiritually; work is doing everything, working everything out in your head with your imagination to get an understanding, and walking by that. You can change by practice; again, keep in mind if the other person is walking in the flesh or hasn't learned how to walk in the spirit in an area. We should restore that person with a humble spirit. This doesn't mean that they will stop right away; give it time. Remember, it's about learning how to walk in the spirit and create from your spirit (**Gal. 6:1**).

9

THE TRUE VALUE OF THINGS

Words of life, His Word of faith will keep you from the evil words that live in the unbelievers' sickness and diseases. No illness can live in the presence of the authority of God in His Word when it's in you. Keep this in your mind: God is where His word is! The Bible tells it this way. Read these verses: *Romans 7* (chapter) and *8:8*. All the words of God are laws; they work every time when walking in the spirit. The law of life and everything pertaining to life comes out of the treasure of His belief in the heart. *Isaiah 55:11 says, "So shall My word be that goeth forth out of My mouth: It shall not return unto Me void, but it shall accomplish that which I please, and it shall prosper in the thing whereto I sent it."*

All we need to do is to fill our hearts with God's Word and see God work His word in us and *through* us. Our joy and peace walks with confidence in God's Word; be prideful of His Word in you. There is nothing more valuable than words of righteousness and truth. "The words that I speak unto you, they are spirit, and they are life." Look at this scripture in *Mark 16:16, 17*: "He that "believeth" and is baptized shall be saved; but he that "believeth" not shall be damned." **Think.** This is God's Word. He has given us the right to use His Word. When words of life are released, there is no word as powerful and evil spirits, and evil spirits of people, have to obey.

People. This is about believing in the authority that Jesus had and has given to the believer; everything is done in His name. He will do the work; our job is to read, study, and believe what the Word of God said about Him *(Matt. 8:16)*, Look deeper into this verse: Jesus cast out the evil-unclean spirit with His Word. The true power is God's words of life. Let's go back to the Garden of Eden where all of this started with words and knowledge; man-made religion, what is considered the religion of man?

The devil was in the serpent. The old ways of humans cause us to never learn for ourselves what God said about what was lawful and what was not. Those trees were put on the earth for a reason! The answer, the *reason* for them, was in the Tree of Life *(Gen, 2:9)*. Anti-knowledge of the tree of good and evil toward God and His laws of peace was forbidden. The relationship the Father desires for all His children is one-on-one, so that we can get to know Him for ourselves and have a personal relationship with our loving Father. Every one of His children is special to Him; you can't have a special, intimate, truthful relationship with someone by the words of others. The devil is described as cunning, wily, or crafty: he is characterized by mental acuteness or penetration. This gives us a look into the heart of the people the devil will use to deceive God's people. We see a lot of this in our churches today. This is why it's so important to read and ask the Lord to give you understanding. The life is in the words "respect," "relationship," and "value." Love the Lord God above any and all things.

Work is a big part of believing: everything involves work spiritually, physically, and mentally. All that has been purchased by the cross was by the works of Jesus *(Gen. 2:2)*. How do you value anything under the laws of sin? You don't learn how to value life from the world's knowledge of good and evil. This scripture will give you some enlightenment: *Romans 8:8*.

Laws are made up of words. Remember that everything in this life is run by (words-laws). God's Word is law because He is God; there is no one bigger than Him. We are creating from what has already been created. Words of life are fighting against words of sin and death. *Roman 6 and 7 (Chapter)* explains a lot about this subject; these verses cover some of what I was talking about:

> *[20] Now if I do that which I would not do, it is no more I that do it, but sin that dwelleth in me. [21] I find then a law*

that, when I would do good, evil is present with me. ²² For I delight in the law of God according to the inward man. ²³ But I see another law in my members, warring against the law of my mind and bringing me into captivity to the law of sin which is in my members.

The most important thing in this life is not money or gold; all the substances of the earth can't equal the words of life and the laws of life (*Prov. 2: 2)*. There are many scriptures that cover this point. You need to learn how to separate old religious words that have no power to affect your situation or your problems. Words of life answer all things: faith and grace-filled words. When you hear words of life, "peace" stores them in the treasury of your heart. Look at *Proverbs 2*. It talks about seeking, crying after, searches through words of deception. Words of life that tell you and me that it will not be easily found. All Scripture teaches us who Christ is in us: "I can do all things through Christ who strengthens me," for the abundance of the heart his mouth speaks. "Jesus said my words are spirit and they are life." Again, we need to be around words that minister God's Word to us, encourage us, strengthen us, and cause us to think positively, words that speak to our spirit and not our flesh. We are to speak words of faith, what God can do in us, through us, and for others. Again, we need to study the Word of God. You are saved and born again, but your flesh still has old, sinful habits that need to be removed. You will have to recreate, with your imagination, from the old ways of the flesh, to line up with God's way and belief.

10
PRACTICE, BECOME HABITS, BECOME LAWS

U nderstanding of the Word: "*but the mouth of the foolish is near destruction.*" The wealth that is hidden in knowledge is the truth; this is our search! Remember the scripture in *James 3:11-18*. We must respect God and His Word. These are our treasures; so many of us have lost our first love of our commandments of love. *Mark 4:3 says:*

> *We begin at the third verse Hearken; Behold, there went out a sower to sow: The teacher is talking about words, words are being spoken to the listener, but some words are not received right away for different reasons, some receive but the word had no root. 5 And some fell on stony ground...*

I made certain that certain laws are a part of my life in my home. Words of doubt and unbelief are not spoken out of my mouth in my home (*Prov. 4:4*). Unless we take the time to meditate (harvest), go over with a fine-tooth comb or gather in the information we have received from our listening of God's Word, nothing of value will ever come to the surface for our decision to believe; to be a strong believer, everything must be established in agreement so you are able to back-up verse by verse. You must take the time to harvest your crops!

"The truth will set you free." Unless you are able to bring in a crop or crops from your labor, you're not free. The truth about who you were created to be, to have, and who you are is hidden in knowledge, and your laboring; seeking, and searching for the truth that is hidden in the knowledge you have received. In your practice acting to build a godly habit, remember that nothing can happen without focus *(Phil. 4:8)*. Think and focus your attention on these things: The weak in faith, the strong in faith, and a baby in the Lord will be considered to be weak because their beliefs are more in the direction of the old nature in things they can see of this world *(Romans 14:22,23; Roman 4:20)*. Walking in the meat of the Word *(Heb. 5:14)*. Strong and weak are linked up to the inward and the outward man *(2 Cor. 4:16 and 1 Sam. 16:7)*.

This inward spiritual man is being renewed day-by-day. He is a baby that has never grown up spiritually *(Heb. 5:13)*. From our old nature of this world, we have made the knowledge of this world our treasures. Now we have to "build" trust in the Word of God, which we don't have an understanding of; all understanding comes from the Lord Jesus. The world believes without true understanding. We operate and do things on our understanding of certain verses, and we get stagnated because we lack understanding of spiritual laws. Work always comes first, then understanding; again, when it comes to learning to ride a bicycle, you first study and then try to ride as you try, and studying understanding comes. If we give these words some consideration, we will discover God's true spiritual meaning of these words; remember, everything come by practice, and in practice, you uncover layers of new understanding that are hidden deep into the thickness of practicing, rehearsing, and action. As I acted out my role of a loving, kind, and considerate husband, there are new habits that are being born. I am thinking of the word "tricks," and learning new tricks, acting out new roles, in my role in this play-movie of the life of Jesus. Think about it. When meeting someone for the first time, we create with our imagination, and we rehearse everything in our mind by contemporary English Version (CEV). Philippians 1:21 *says, "If I live, it will be for Christ, and if I die, I will gain even more. Romans 14:8 For whether we live, we live unto the Lord; and whether we die, we die unto the Lord. Whether we live therefore or die, we are the Lord's."*

We were created to be responsible for everything concerning our lives. The knowledge of sin of the flesh doesn't teach that; to be a responsible person, you must practice downloading it into your spirit. Say "I am a responsible person," then look for things to be responsible for. It begins with the words you choose to believe by repeating them over and over to yourself. Once a word come across your path, you must make a decision about what to do with that word you hear. You must take responsibility for that word to have any change. You are being responsible for the wrong things if you are going to see or have any improvement. Come to terms with the <u>fact</u> that there is a good and a bad, the reward for doing right and punishment for doing wrong.

You can learn anything, and you have the creative ability to learn to achieve whatever you decide to go after. Do you believe that by practice you can do anything? The problem we have *is* the practice part because practice requires *work*. Deception, and being deceived, all work positively or negatively if you're going in the right direction, or the wrong direction; you will have to work at it. Spiritual practice happens when your will and your emotions put words to work from within you and your imagination. Working at being lazy, procrastination, frustrated, fighting, and thinking about giving up, is part of becoming better (Rev. 3:12). "Him that overcometh..." John 5: 1-9 says, *"⁴ For an angel went down at a certain season into the pool and troubled the water. Whosoever then first stepped in, after the troubling of the water, was made whole of whatsoever disease he had."*

Think about giving up frustration, anger, and disappointment, year-after-year; practice being committed and dedicated. Without these two words, you can never achieve whatever you are going after. The more you give into laziness and procrastination, the more difficult it will be to come out of it. Think of words as tools that the Creator has given us to do the "work" that is needed.

Let us go back to what I said about "value." Before going into anything, it could be a home, a business, or a relationship. What will be the "things/words" that you will make valuable? Your treasure: this is why we first seek the valuables of the "kingdom:" truth, faith, and understanding. God's Words are valuable, but until they become valuable to us, they have no value. You are seeking, searching, for a valuable understanding of what the Word of God is talking about.

Practice Acting, Becomes Habit, Becomes Law

    I am emotional and passionate about prayer because I know the value of prayer, and that it works. I am emotional and passionate when studying the Bible because I know that I learn a lot from reading. There is nothing more important than educating yourself about the kingdom of Heaven, and truth. Husbands and wives, rehearse your plays and words to say to each other; keep this in your thinking: you are building your character by practice. This is our treasure. Remember what was said: "Out of a man's heart, he speaks words that are good." *Proverbs 10:14 says, "Wise men lay up knowledge"* (in the treasure of their heart, so He can bring in a harvest of life.)

THE END

Printed in the USA
CPSIA information can be obtained
at www.ICGtesting.com
LVHW020026161024
793941LV00003B/24